The Parents' Guide to Surviving the College Admissions Process

The Parents' Guide to Surviving the College Admissions Process

Ellen Fitzpatrick Pinkman
and
Barbara Trecker

A CITADEL PRESS BOOK
Published by Carol Publishing Group

A Citadel Press Book
Published by Carol Publishing Group
Citadel Press is a registered trademark of Carol Communications, Inc.

Editorial, sales and distribution, rights and permissions inquiries should be addressed to Carol Publishing Group, 120 Enterprise Avenue, Secaucus, N.J. 07094.

In Canada: Canadian Manda Group, One Atlantic Avenue, Suite 105, Toronto, Ontario M6K 3E7.

Carol Publishing Group books may be purchased in bulk at special discounts for sales promotion, fund-raising, or educational purposes. Special editions can be created to specifications. For details, contact Special Sales Department, 120 Enterprise Avenue, Secaucus, N.J. 07094.

Manufactured in the United States of America
10 9 8 7 6 5 4 3 2 1

Library of Congress Cataloging-in-Publication Data

Pinkman, Ellen Fitzpatrick.
    The parents' guide to surviving the college admissions process / Ellen Fitzpatrick Pinkman, Barbara Trecker.
        p. cm.
    Rev. ed. of: Help! c1994.
    "A Citadel Press book."
    ISBN 0-8065-1825-1 (pbk.)
    1. Universities and colleges—United States—Admission. 2. College choice—United States.   I. Trecker, Barbara.   II. Pinkman, Ellen Fitzpatrick. Help!   III. Title.
LB2351.2.P567   1996
378.1'05'0973—dc20   96–41724
                                                                              CIP

To our children,

Molly, Katie, Sophie and Carrie,

who caused just enough trouble along the way

to inspire us to write this book,

but who came through in the end,

as they always do.

Contents

Acknowledgments

We wish to thank the following individuals who read the manuscript at various stages, made helpful suggestions, and encouraged us to keep going: Karen "the sprout" Brooks, Sandy McGarry, Carol McKinney, David Rosen, Linda Rosen, Zvi Sabin, Mark Scala, and Linda Steuerwald.

We also want to thank our husbands, Neil Pinkman and Jim Trecker, for cheering us on.

A special thanks to all the parents, teachers, guidance counselors, and school administrators who loved our first edition and spread the good word. Their support, along with that of countless book store owners, book reviewers, and others, made this second edition a reality.

Most of all, we want to thank our children, Molly and Sophie Trecker and Katie and Carrie Pinkman, for giving us a reason to write this book and for providing us with all the crazy, but true, stories.

Finally, we want to thank our children's friends and their parents, for sharing their experiences with us.

Meet the Kids

Here are some of the kids you'll meet in this book.

Dan
Northwestern
University

Carrie
Boston
College

Katie
Rutgers
College

Mike
Syracuse
University

Molly
University of
Michigan

Sophie
University of
Wisconsin

Ryan
Wesley
College

The Parents' Guide to Surviving the College Admissions Process

Your Kid Needs You

*T*he first thing a parent must realize about today's college admissions process is that it's a whole different ball game from when *you* went to college. The process has become bigger, longer and more complex. Beyond that, kids are different today, and so are parents.

When we went to school thirty years ago, we basically handled the entire process by ourselves. Sure, we discussed our choices with our parents, but we did the research, we sent away for the applications, and we filled them out by ourselves; our parents probably never even looked them over. We applied to a total of two or three colleges. We took the SATs only once; we didn't take any spe-

*T*hink of this book as a how-to guide for parents of college-bound students. We'll take you step-by-step. We'll tell you what to do when, and how to get your child involved. You can do it!

cial courses to prepare for them, and while we knew they were important, we didn't believe that our future success in life depended solely on our SAT scores.

Compare that with today's college admissions process. Most students apply to at least six colleges. They take standardized tests, two, three, even four times. They start worrying a lot earlier, but that doesn't mean they take any action. Of course, there are some supermotivated kids who figure out the process and do what they're supposed to do, ahead of time. But most kids, although they *want* to go to college, don't seem to be able to get their act together and thus delay starting the whole process.

"Where do you want to go to college?" we have asked any number of high school juniors.

"Any place that will take me," Carrie said.

"Have you sent away for any information? Have you visited any colleges?"

"Nah," said Ryan.

And this from bright, obviously college-bound students. Our own personal theory is that the process has become so overwhelming that a kid's way of dealing with it is by *not* dealing with it. Avoidance is the path of least resistance.

The process *is* complex and it *can* be confusing. But, armed with the right information, a parent can perform the vital role of steering his or her child through the maze. You can do this a lot better than your child's friends; better even than your child's guidance counselor. (That's a whole other story. See chapter 9.)

The truth is, your kids need your help. They may not realize it, and even if they do, they certainly would never admit it. But you *can* make a real difference.

This book is intended to give you the information you need to really help your child through the process. It's based on scores of interviews with high school and college students, parents, guidance counselors, college admissions officers and others. It's a practical, real-life guide. It not only tells you about things such as rolling admissions and registering for standardized tests, but, probably more important, it tells you what to do to get your kid to write the essay and how to avoid screaming matches during the college visit. (What would *you* do if you drove 300 miles to visit a college and your daughter refused to get out of the car because, as she put it, "Look at the shoes those kids are wearing. I'd never go to a school where kids wear shoes like that.")

Think of this book as a how-to guide for parents of college-bound students. We're going to take you step by step. We'll give you timetables and helpful hints. We'll hold your hand. We've been through it, so we know what works and what doesn't. Most of all, this isn't one of those goody two-shoes books that assumes your child is going to be motivated and cooperative. We know what kids are like in the real world (God help us) and we'll give you strategies for dealing with those ugly realities.

Don't worry. It'll be fun.

Take Charge

*H*ere's the first great truth of this book and probably the single most important thing you need to know: TAKE CHARGE.

By taking charge we mean making the decision that you will become actively involved in the process, that you may even have to take the lead. That's okay. Don't wait for your kid to take action or even to ask you for help. It may not happen, and if it ever does, it may be too late. It's not a crime to take the controls and shout out a few orders along the way.

However, taking charge doesn't mean that you do it all, even if you think you can do it better, quicker, and with less hassle. You know your kid, and you've got to strike the right balance.

*M*ake a decision to become actively involved in the college admissions process. Take charge, if you have to. Get involved and stay involved, and ten-to-one your kid will come around.

Here's an example of taking charge

When Katie was a junior in high school, we started talking about colleges and we gently suggested that she should perhaps send away for some information. Days passed; weeks passed; months passed. We nagged her mercilessly; we went so far as to put a standard letter in the computer. All she had to do was change the addresses and print them out. Nothing! No action. Yet we persisted. We were under the mistaken notion that if she didn't care enough to make that small effort, then what did that mean about her desire to go to college? We believed that her failure to send out those letters meant she didn't deserve to go to college.

Will you please stop bugging me? I swear I'll send away for the information tomorrow! Honest!

Finally, we broke down and realized it was time to take action. We looked up the phone numbers and spent about a half hour one day calling the colleges and requesting information. (No, you don't need to disguise your voice so the college will think you're the student. This did cross our minds, however. So intimidating is this process that many parents actually think the person who answers the phone will make a notation next to your child's name, saying, "Parent called for info; child obviously lacks interest." It doesn't happen that way. What does happen is that your child's name goes into a computer and then you're basically set. He or she will get ongoing communications from the school; some schools will even automatically send an application when the time is right.)

The point here is that instead of spending hours yelling at your kid to take some action, there are times when you should just do it yourself. It doesn't mean your kid is unmotivated or doesn't deserve to go to college. It means that you're being helpful and supportive. Remember, it's probably not that your kid doesn't care. On the other hand, he or she probably cares too much. So don't be afraid to jump in. But, of course, don't do any of this without his or her knowledge.

The road ahead

Planning for college should start in earnest the summer before the student's junior year in high school. (That may be a bit compulsive. Don't panic if you get into the process later.) That means you're facing about a year and a half of *stuff:* all through junior year and most of senior year. You're going to have your ups and downs during that time. You no doubt will experience many times when you absolutely want to kill your kid. You'll probably want to shoot the guidance counselor as well. You'll want to tear your hair out. But if you're armed with the right information, if you plan ahead, and if you're willing to take a really active role, you'll be surprised at how smooth and successful the process can be. You may even enjoy it! Believe it or not, you'll actually miss it when you've gotten your last kid into college. We have a friend whose only child is now a junior in college, yet each year he buys the new college guides and keeps them handy, thumbing through them wistfully.

Why do you think we're writing this book, anyway?

Becoming an Expert

ore than 2,000 schools are profiled in the college guide *Peterson's Four Year Colleges*. Which one is right for your son or daughter? Well, the first thing to remember is that there's not just one school that's right for anyone. There are dozens. That's right. There are dozens of schools at which your child will not only get a good education but, more important, be happy. And, better news yet, your kid will be able to get into most of these schools. The trick is selecting those schools that provide a good match in terms of academics, size, location, cost, and lots of other preferences.

This chapter is going to tell you how to find out about col-

*R*ead, talk, ask questions. Go to the library. Browse through bookstores. Make lists. Get organized. Immerse yourself in college information. Some of it will rub off on your kid.

leges and how to start narrowing down the choices so that you end up with a manageable list of schools that you'll both want to take a closer look at.

The entire point of this book is that you *can* become an expert and help guide your child through the process. But there are some parents who have neither the time nor the temperament for the task. If you are one of these parents, perhaps you should consider hiring a private consultant. This is like having your very own personal guidance counselor, who will help your child with everything from selecting possible schools to filling out applications.

Before signing on with a private consultant, check costs, credentials, and references. Make sure you understand exactly what you are getting for the fee. Private consultants are usually quite expensive. Does the fee include help in filling out applications, filing for financial aid, and writing the required essays?

My Sundays are ruined now with all this college stuff.

Even if you decide to hire a private consultant, keep reading this book. After all, it's your kid and you'll still need to be well informed.

Talk to your kid

The most important thing to remember is that it's the kids who are going to school, not the parents. Of course, you know your child better than anyone, but sometimes what you want for them isn't what they want for themselves. Talk to them. Find out what they're thinking. But do this casually. Remember what we said earlier about the pressures kids are feeling? When Dan was a high school junior, his weekends were ruined, he said, because "Sunday is college day at my house." Don't make a big formal thing out of it. Just slip it in casually. If your kid's not in the mood to talk when you are, skip it. When we kept forcing the issue with Carrie, she started referring to college talk as "The Big C" and refused to participate. Take your signals from your child.

Get in the car

One good way to get your child motivated to start thinking

Joe goes to Duke. He says the parties are really cool.

about schools is to visit a nearby campus. Now, this isn't the same as "The College Trip," which we'll talk about in chapter 5. This is a real easy, casual, fun, "Let's take a drive and look around" type of trip. As you probably know, this or any trip will work better if a friend comes along. Go when classes are in session, because any campus is more appealing when it's filled with kids. Don't have a set agenda – no information sessions, no visits to classes. Just wander around, get a snack in the student union, and definitely drop a few bucks in the bookstore. Drink in the college atmosphere.

Immerse yourself

The best way to learn about colleges, and the college admissions process, is to talk to everyone. Remember, you're not the first parent going through this. Take advantage of those who have already been through the process. Talk to friends, relatives, other kids, kids' parents, everyone.

Find out where other students from your child's school have gone. Some high schools will provide a list from past graduating classes of where each student went or, better yet, a list of what schools each student was accepted at, along with that student's standardized test scores and class ranking (names deleted, of course). That starts to give you an idea of the academic expectations of specific colleges.

The next best way to get information is reading. READ EVERYTHING YOU CAN GET YOUR HANDS ON. Read the education stories in the newspaper. Many magazines, such as *U.S. News and World Report* and *Money* magazine, for instance, come out with an annual rating of colleges. These are valuable because they provide the most current information.

Be aware of general news that may affect your child's college choices. For example, when Molly wanted to apply to Berkeley, the newspaper articles we had read about serious cutbacks to education in California because of the state's budget crunch made us wonder about Berkeley's future viability. McGill, a fine school in Montreal and a relatively good buy for Americans, has to be seen in the light of the French separatist movement in Canada and what that might mean for an English university in the heart of French Canada. No, you don't have to get a Ph.D. in current events, but you do have to be aware, and you have to understand how the political, economic, and social environment could affect your child's college plans.

Hey, that big college guide came in handy today. I used it to kill a spider.

Go to any bookstore, head for the section on college guides, and look at what's available. Buy at least one overall guide to colleges, such as *Peterson's* or *Lovejoy's College Guide* – the kind that lists every four-year college in the country along with its vital statistics: cost, number of students, entrance difficulty, average standardized test scores and class standing, list of majors, financial aid, athletics, housing, etc., etc. If for no other reason, buy this book because it will give you addresses and phone numbers. This will be your bible. Keep it handy at all times, and flip through it frequently. DO NOT, under any circumstances, hand it to your son or daughter and say, "Here, pick a college." Instead, leave it out somewhere. Eventually – eventually – your child will pick up the book and start to use it.

In addition to the big guide, you may want to get one of the more fun books that will probably appeal more to your kid than to you – the kind of book that rates not only the academics, but the dating scene and the pizza places. Two such books are *Lisa Birnbach's Guide to Colleges* – this book will tell you what the school's gay scene is like and where the best student hang-outs are – and *The Insider's Guide to the Colleges.*

Visit the library. They've got all the books, plus catalogs and information from the colleges themselves. The guidance office at the high school has lots of information on file, too. Most will have college guides, as well as brochures and videos from individual colleges. (By the way, it's not a bad idea to start to make yourself known at the guidance office. More on this in chapter 9.)

Make a checklist

In order to make the task of selecting colleges more manageable, make up a checklist with different variables. This will make it easier to start discussing preferences. Here's a sample of what to consider:

Cost:

- **State schools** tend to cost a lot less than private.
- **Private schools** in the Northeast are usually the most expensive.

Academics:

Time to be realistic about your kid's performance in high school: grade point average, class rank, standardized test scores. But when you're doing this, remember that demographics are on your side. There simply aren't as many high school seniors around today as there were twenty years ago. In fact, the numbers are at an all time low. That means we're in a buyer's market, as far as colleges go. There are fewer kids looking to get into more schools. College admissions officers themselves admit that it's easier to get into their schools today than it was fifteen or twenty years ago. Now, this doesn't apply to the very top schools, which remain extremely competitive. But it does apply to just about all other schools that fall below that rarefied Ivy League atmosphere. So that's definitely good news.

Size:

- **Small** *(under 2,000 students)*
- **Medium** *(2,000 – 10,000)*
- **Large** *(over 10,000)*

Location:

- **Close** *enough so your kid can come home on weekends*

- **Far enough** *so that you can't visit him or her all the time*
- **Really far** *(at least a plane ride) away*

Setting:

- **Urban, rural, college town,** *etc.*

Type:

- **Private vs. state supported**
- **Co–ed vs. same sex** *(a dying breed)*
- **College vs. university** *(usually larger and with substantial graduate programs)*
- **Religious affiliated vs. secular**

Other preferences:

- *Does your kid want to live away from home or commute?*
- *Is he or she interested in a particular major?*
- *Are sports a serious consideration?*
- *What about performing arts?*

After you've been at all this a while, the next step is to make a big list – maybe twenty or twenty-five schools that seem to fit the criteria you (and hopefully your kid) have selected. Divide these schools into three groups:

Long Shots :

They sound great but it would be kind of a miracle if your kid got in.

Good Shots:

Given your kid's performance, these schools should accept him or her.

Sure Shots:

These are the safeties. One thing about the safeties: there's no point in keeping them on the list unless your child feels he or she could be happy going there.

The purpose of this list is to give some order to your thoughts and preferences and to those of your child. It will probably change a lot over the next few months; you'll both be dropping and adding schools. But it will help both of you to get something down on paper. Don't underestimate how much your child's thinking may change over the course of this process. Sometimes kids who start out thinking they want a Big Ten atmosphere, for instance, end up realizing they would be happier at a much smaller school. So make sure there's some variety on the list. And certainly don't let your child pin all his or her hopes on one school.

Let's talk for a minute about special talents, such as athletic ability, that can make your child a more attractive applicant to colleges. Being an all-state athlete often turns a long shot into a good shot. Depending upon how big a tennis or track star your child is, he or she may be wooed by college coaches – and they can be very aggressive. College coaches *do* have a certain amount of influence with Admissions, but they don't have the final say. No matter what a coach might promise, there's *no guarantee* of admission. Keep that in mind when the attention starts to get overwhelming.

When compiling your list of colleges, the guidance office can be helpful. Your child should discuss his or her preferences with guidance and then have guidance do a computer search for appropriate matches.

Now you've got this big list of possibilities. It's time to take a closer look. Send away for information from the colleges you have selected. (If your child has already taken the PSATs, you were probably inundated with catalogs. Select any material that is of interest.)

When sending away for information, it doesn't matter what you ask for; the college will send its standard prospective applicant's package: a viewbook or catalog, perhaps even an application.

Here's how to proceed. Either call or send a postcard requesting information. Sure, try to get your kid to do this. But if a couple of weeks go by and nothing happens, just do it yourself, as we said before. The big college guide will have telephone numbers and addresses. Soon you will be flooded with stuff – gorgeous, slick, color viewbooks that will make any college look great. Many schools even have videos available. If your child will take a look at these, he or she may start to get excited, because the materials make the places look great. The viewbooks and videos are useful for giving you a feel for the place, but remember, they're sales pieces. You'll also want information from less biased sources, such as guidance counselors and independent college guides.

As you're gathering this information, designate a visible place – like a corner of a room, not just a drawer or a cabinet – to store the *stuff*. Again, having this material out and visible is a subtle prod to your child.

Organize the stuff

At this point, it is very easy to get completely flooded and overwhelmed with information, so make sure you get and stay organized. Here are a couple of helpful tools to help you do so.

First, the GRID. This is a way for you to see, at a glance, all the important information you need to know about each school. *(We've prepared a grid for you. It appears on pages 34-35. Just lay this book face down on a copier to get one or more copies for use.)*

> I spilled soda on the grid. Any chance you have another copy?

The grid should list the name of the school and the pertinent information: address, telephone number, college code, cost (tuition plus room and board), number of students, average SAT/ACT scores, deadlines, and whether SAT-IIs (formerly called Achievement tests) are required. Personalize the grid according to your needs and what's important to your child: the male/female ratio, perhaps, or the in-state/out-of-state ratio. Leave space for later in the process to check whether you've ordered an application, had test scores sent, and received confirmation that the completed application was received by the school. At the top of the grid, put the student's social security number. It's the first question colleges will ask, and it becomes the student's ID number for all inquiries and correspondence. Also include the high school code, which is needed on applications and test registration forms.

This grid is going to get a lot of use – ours was in shreds by the end of the process. Make a couple of copies, because you don't want to lose it. Stick one up on the refrigerator, or on the wall behind the phone at home. Take another copy to work, because you'll probably be making phone calls from the office.

The grid and all the information on it can also be put on a computer spreadsheet, if that's easier for you.

Second, start making FILE FOLDERS to hold the information from those schools that you are really interested in. At first, you'll stick in the brochures and catalogs. Then you'll stick in the applications as they come, the copies of the completed applications, the canceled checks, all other correspondence. YOU REALLY NEED THESE FOLDERS. Keep them in a safe but accessible place. Your kid's room is probably *not* the wisest choice, for reasons we're sure you can understand.

Narrow down your list

As you go through this process, you'll start to narrow down the list somewhat. Keep talking, keep reading, maybe start to take some college trips. By this time, believe it or not, your kid will probably start to get into it. He or she will offer some opinions. You'll start to get a feel for what they're thinking and what their preferences are. But don't be discouraged if they're still in the noncommittal stage. And don't be concerned if their preferences are based on idiotic reasons. For instance, Molly absolutely refused to consider any school that was "near the Great Lakes." (She ended up at the University of Michigan.) Erica would apply only to colleges whose school colors appealed to her. Some kids won't apply to a school if certain other kids apply there. Sophie actually had a thing about the color of the bricks in the buildings. And the mascot: it had to be an actual animal. (She liked Indiana University, but never quite made her peace with the Hoosier mascot.) These are the times when it is very important to stay cool. These notions will pass.

Live with your list

By the spring of your kid's junior year, you should have a list of between ten and twenty schools. Live with the list; talk about the schools with anyone who will listen; add schools, drop schools. Keep refining your list. Remember, if your kid is like most, he or she will probably apply to between six and ten schools, so that's the number you're aiming for. (By the way, most application fees range from $10 to $50, so it does make some sense to limit the list.)

Now you have a really workable list – perhaps ten or twelve schools that both you and your child feel comfortable with. Make sure the list is balanced and includes some long shots, some good shots, and some sure shots. Make a revised grid if necessary.

The next big challenge is getting a handle on the application process – what to do, and when. It's a lot more complicated than it used to be.

Understanding the Process

By now you've immersed yourself in college information, you've started getting organized, and you've filled out the all-important grid. It's time to get started. Now we're going to give you a general overview of the actual application process – what needs to be done, when it must be done, and who should do it.

When we parents went through this twenty to thirty years ago as students, things were quite different. None of us really got serious about college applications until after Christmas of our senior year. Today, many seniors already have an acceptance by Christmas, or even earlier. Although the general rule is still January or February

*M*ake sure you get organized early. The more you under- stand about the process, the more likely you'll have smooth sailing through the months ahead.

for the application deadline, with notification in mid–April, there are important exceptions, and these exceptions are becoming more numerous. The point is, START EARLY.

Rolling right along

If you have looked through your big college guide, you probably noticed, under deadlines, that some schools indicated *rolling*. Rolling admissions means that the college will review the student's application as soon as it is complete, make a decision, and notify the student of that decision. These colleges, mostly the large state universities as well as some others, process the applications as they come in, on a continuous basis. Other colleges wait until the deadline is past, when they have all the applications in hand, and then make their decisions and notify all students at the same time.

If your child is interested in a school with rolling admissions, the application should be in as early in the senior year as possible. That means requesting an application early, certainly by July before the senior year. Many of these colleges start to send out applications in August, and most say they will accept completed applications after September 1. THE EARLIER THE APPLICATION IS IN, THE BETTER YOUR CHILD'S CHANCES OF BEING ACCEPTED.

For example, Penn State, a mammoth educational system with 30,000 undergraduates spread over twenty-two campuses, puts it this way: If you get your application in early, you will have a better chance of being admitted to the University Park campus – the main and most coveted campus in the system. The same application, if it arrives later in the year, even though it's still well ahead of the deadline, will have a tougher time. Indiana University in Bloomington accepts applications during the summer before senior year and may even notify students before September.

Most schools that offer rolling admissions let the student know his or her status within three to six weeks after receipt of the application. It's a great feeling for a student to have an acceptance under his or her belt early in the year; it's a real morale booster.

Unfortunately, many guidance offices are not geared up for the demands of rolling admissions. They're still in a time warp that makes them think crunch time is December and January. So be prepared to pester the guidance office to make sure they have class ranks ready early (these are needed for the application) and to make sure they do their part to complete the application.

Many schools (including all the Ivy Leagues) have an *early decision* option. This is for students who are absolutely sure where they want to go. If they submit their application by a specified, early deadline, the school will notify them early, usually in November or December, as opposed to the standard notification date in April. Students may apply for early decision to only one school, and, if accepted, the student must withdraw any applications submitted to other schools and accept the offer of admission. This is actually called *binding early decision*. A few other schools – the University of North Carolina is one of them – offer *nonbinding early decision*, sometimes also referred to as *early acceptance* or *early notification*. They'll let your child know early if he or she is accepted, but the student doesn't have to agree to go there. There may be other variations; each school's rules should be checked carefully.

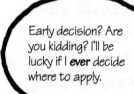

Early decision? Are you kidding? I'll be lucky if I **ever** decide where to apply.

Colleges that offer early decision will either accept the student, reject at that point, or throw the application back into the pool for consideration at the normal deadline, depending on its strength. Most colleges say that their standards for early decision are higher than for regular admission. However, they add that if you are denied early decision, that will not affect your chances of regular admission.

If early decision is a consideration for your child, it requires advance planning and an accelerated time schedule, just like rolling admissions.

Another option which might be right for some students is *early admission*. These are for the students who apply for college admission directly after the junior year. This takes lots of individual planning, so talk to guidance and the prospective colleges very early in the process.

Avoid the last-minute rush in guidance

Even if your child's schools don't have rolling admissions, and even if he or she is not interested in early decision, it still makes sense to get the applications in early anyway. The guidance counselor will have more time to deal with applications in October or November than in December or January, when all the last-minute applications come flooding in.

What's the big hurry? It's only Christmas. These applications aren't due till February.

Because so many applications are submitted early these days, senior year grades are not really a factor in the admissions decision at many colleges, although those schools which notify in April will of course look at the first semester senior grades. Junior year grades are very important. Many admissions officers say they like to see an upward trend in grades over the high school years.

Course selection, especially in the senior year, is extremely important. Colleges want to see a challenging course schedule senior year, including advanced placement and honors classes. Check specific college requirements regarding the number of years of high school English, math, science, and foreign language required.

What's included in the application

When we talk about the application, we mean a lot more than the booklet that gets filled out. The APPLICATION actually has several components. First there's the application form itself, which usually has two parts, one that's filled out by the student and one that's filled out by the guidance office. Then there's the essay, which may or may not be required but is always a good idea. Then there are the letters of recommendation, the test score reports, and the interview, maybe.

Let's take a little closer look at each of these.

The application

Most applications have two parts: one to be completed by the student, and one to be completed by the guidance office. (We'll go into the details of the application later, in chapter 7.) The important point here is that *you* need to shepherd the process through the guidance office. The student fills out his or her part of the application and then either sends that in to the college or gives it, along with the part to be filled out by the guidance office, to the guidance counselor, who supplies the transcript, class rank, personal comments, etc. *Follow up with the guidance department and make sure the application goes out as soon as possible.*

Standardized tests

Find out what standardized tests are required by your colleges, and enter this information on your grid. Most colleges require the Scholastic Assessment Test (SAT, formerly the Scholastic Aptitude Test; more on that later), or, in some parts of the country, the American College Testing program test (ACT). Some, usually the most selective, also require the SAT-II tests, formerly called Achievement tests. Get the schedule of the SATs from the guidance office or from the College Board Admissions Testing Program, administered through the Educational Testing Service, P.O. Box 6200, Princeton, NJ, 08541–6200. Registration information about the ACT can be obtained from: ACT Registration, P.O. Box 414, Iowa City, IA, 52243–0414. The tests are offered only on certain dates and at certain test locations. You have to register well in advance or risk paying extra fees, not getting your preferred testing site, or being shut out of the test entirely. Most college-bound students take the SATs several times during their junior and senior years. If your child is applying to a school with rolling admissions or early decision, he or she has to take them in the junior year, or the score reports will hold up the application. Plan out the best schedule for testing early in the junior year, and make sure you don't miss any of the registration deadlines.

SAT scores are reported directly to your child, to the high school guidance office, and to any colleges you specify. Most applications have a place, to be filled in by the guidance office, with the test scores. *But colleges also require direct reporting of the scores from the Educational Testing Service.*

We'll talk a lot more about SATs and ACTs in chapter 6, but for now just be aware that they are an important part of the application process and you have to plan for them early.

The interview

Some schools require interviews as part of the application process, some just suggest them, and others do not offer them. Find out and plan early. Many schools that recommend interviews have only a limited number of appointments available.

Interviews are usually conducted on campus, so it's a good idea to try to coincide the interview with the campus visit, especially if the school is not nearby. Some schools will arrange interviews with students even before the application is received.

Many schools also offer interviews at various other locations

What if they ask me what books I've read?

throughout the country. Find out when the interviewers will be in your area, and set up an appointment.

Still another alternative is the alumni interview. Many schools have an active alumni network spread out all over the country. This network is made up of graduates who are still so gung-ho about their college that they volunteer to interview prospective students in their area. From the student's

perspective, these are the easiest to handle. At Molly's alumni interview for the
University of Michigan, the interviewer
spent the entire time convincing her what
a great school it was.

Do you think that lady I babysat for two summers ago might give me a letter of recommendation?

The decision about whether to
pursue an interview is very individual. Let's
face it, some kids do a lot better in these
situations than others. If you or your child
thinks it's a good idea, then go for it. Help
your child by doing a practice interview
with him or her, or encourage your child
to do some practice interviews with a
friend. Help your child think up some of
his or her own questions to ask, because the interview is usually a
two-way process. A good question to be prepared to answer is "Why
do you want to come to this school?"

Letters of recommendation

Start planning for letters of recommendation. Some colleges
require them, but it's a good idea to include at least one letter of recommendation with the application whether it's required or not.

Many schools require at least one letter from a teacher or
some other school representative who knows the student very well.
Other possible sources for letters of recommendation are sports
coaches, music teachers, employers, pastors, family friends, etc.

Chances are, anyone your kid feels comfortable enough

to ask for a recommendation will want to say good things. Just make sure the individual is capable of writing a coherent, grammatical letter. A letter filled with misspelled words and incorrect grammar isn't going to help your child's application, no matter what it says.

The essay

And then there's the essay – often the single biggest barrier to getting the applications in early. But that really is a whole other chapter (8).

We'll give you a lot more details about these elements in later chapters. The important point here is timing: start planning early, and do everything you can to convince your child to complete his or her applications early. A good deadline to aim for is to have all applications completed and sent in by Thanksgiving. YOU CAN DO IT! Then all you and your child have to do is sit back and try not to look smug as everyone else is still scrambling around.

Getting the Info

*T*his chapter, which will tell you how to send away for information and applications, is going to be very short because this really is a no–brainer, although it's amazing how many people (us included) get really hung up on this step.

There are four basic ways you can request information:

(1) Have your kid write a very short form letter, saying something like this: "I am a high school junior interested in applying to College X. Please send me some information about the school, and also an application for admission in the fall of ———." If you're sick of waiting for your kid to do this, do it yourself.

(2) Put the same information on a postcard. It's cheaper.

College Address Phone College Code e-mail address	Cost	Number of Students	Application Deadline	Essay Required?	SAT-IIs Required

The Grid

High School Code _____

Average SAT/ACT Scores	Date Application Requested	Application Received	Date Application Delivered to Guidance	Application Received by College	SAT/ACT Scores Received by College	Notes

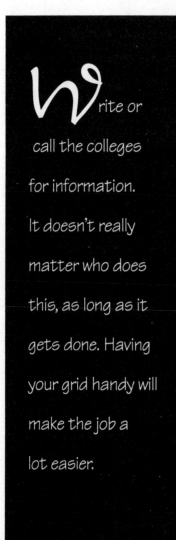

Write or call the colleges for information. It doesn't really matter who does this, as long as it gets done. Having your grid handy will make the job a lot easier.

(3) Ask the high school guidance office for some ready–made postcards. (Most have them.) Just fill in the blanks on the card.

(4) Call the school. This is the method preferred by those neurotic parents who don't always trust the U.S. Postal Service, and who need to hear someone on the other end say, "Okay, we'll send out that information and send the application as soon as it is available."

One thing about calling, however: you won't always get a live voice on the other end. Most of the big schools, which have tens of thousands of applicants, have resorted to elaborate recorded voice mail messages which require you to listen carefully and then press all sorts of buttons on your push-button phone. If you don't like dealing with computers, then make believe you are one of the seven remaining people in the country who still have a rotary dial phone, wait until the end of the recording and stay on the line; a human being will come on.

(5) Surf the net. Many colleges have lots of information available on the internet.

Use your grid!

Whether you're sending for the applications or calling, have your grid handy. If you've filled it out correctly, you'll have all the addresses and phone numbers right there; that really makes the job a lot easier. You'll also have your child's social security number handy, and it's always a good idea to include that in any communication with the college, right from the very beginning. Make sure you mark on the grid that the application was ordered, and check it off again when the application is received.

Most of the smaller colleges do have admissions staff readily available to speak directly to you or your child. They are extremely helpful and will answer any and all of your questions. Don't hesitate to make these calls yourself. The college doesn't care if it's talking to the student or the parent. They understand that often students don't get home from school until after their offices close, and that parents usually have more flexibility to make phone calls.

The point to remember is that the colleges are as eager to send you the information as you are to receive it. Remember what we said about the dip in college age demographics and this being a buyer's market.

Can you call for me, Mom? I've got basketball practice after school.

Some more of your college catalogues came today, Dad.

The deluge of information

Once you request information and an application, your child's name will be put into the computer and he or she will probably receive a steady flow of communications from the school.

When the catalog first arrives, your child will have the opportunity to request more specialized information as well, through various return mail postcards. This is when he or she can indicate a special interest in a particular major, sports, performing arts, financial aid info, etc.

Read through the information very carefully. There may be very important, unexpected information. For instance, the University of Wisconsin asks students to apply for college housing during a specific week in October. It's a totally separate process from applying for admission to the school, and, in fact, can take place even before the student applies for admission. Students who don't apply at that time often cannot get college housing. The only way you would know this is by reading the college information packet very carefully.

Applications generally are not ready until late summer for fall admission the following year. Some of the catalogues have applications in them, but make sure they are dated for the correct year. Many schools change their applications from year to year, or at least code them differently. However, old applications do give you and your child a chance to see the type of information required.

If your child has already taken the PSATs or SATs and checked the appropriate box about requesting information from colleges, you will soon be deluged with catalogs. But don't wait for these. As soon as you know the colleges your child is particularly interested in, encourage him or her to send for the information, or do it yourself.

When the material starts arriving, designate a spot in the house for them. For those that make it to the short list (the ones you're both really serious about), prepare folders and keep them handy. Put the name of the school prominently on the tab of the folder, and then store all further correspondence in the appropriate folder.

Remember, don't force your child to read the information as it comes in, and don't be discouraged if your child seems to take absolutely no interest in the material. Just leave it lying around – a good spot is near the TV remote control – and eventually, we promise you, even the most apathetic kid will take a look.

By this point you should really be starting to have fun. Good. Because what comes ahead – the standardized tests, the applica-

tions, including the dreaded essay, and dealing with the guidance office – is probably going to be less fun.

   But before we get into the heavy stuff, it's time to set off on
a college trip.

The CollegeTrip

*T*he college trip can be the absolutely best part of the whole college admissions process. Or it can be pure hell. We've had both kinds.

Just try to remember: *The college trip is supposed to be fun.* Any factual information you learn about the college is a bonus. The college trip is supposed to give the student a "feel" for the place, the kind of information you can't get out of books or catalogs. That means the best time to go is when school is in session. But don't worry if summer is the only time you can go. Most colleges have enough students hanging around in the summer so that you'll still get the full flavor of the place.

College catalogs give you the facts; college trips give you the feel. Try to go when classes are in session. Hang out a while, watch the sights and the sounds, and try to picture your child there.

When you visit a college, it's not necessary to sit in on classes or to see a classroom building or the library. Of course, if your child is a future chemistry major and he or she is just dying to see the chem labs, great. Or if he or she is really into computers, then you might want to make a stop at the computer center. If that's what your child wants to do, fine. But if not, don't force it.

If your kid is like most, then what you'll probably want to do is visit the student union, sample the food in the cafeteria, browse in the bookstore, steal a glimpse of a dorm room, and check out the neighborhood and the downtown shops.

Which colleges should you visit? Obviously, time and budget will dictate just how many schools you can see and how far you can roam. Reserve the college trips for those schools that are on your child's short list. There should be a pretty high degree of interest in the school to begin with, especially if it's far away and the trip will involve a considerable investment in time and money. If there are other schools close by, why not check them out too, even if they're not on your list? You might as well – you can never tell what will turn your kid on. The college trip will either heighten your child's interest or help cross a school off the list. Most kids will have pretty strong opinions based on what they see during the college trip. So a lot is hanging on these trips, and, as a parent, you want to make sure you don't inadvertently mess things up.

The college trip can motivate even the most laid back student

Lots of parents told us that it wasn't until they made their first college trip that their kids started to get serious about the process. That's because the college trip brings it to life. Most colleges look pretty good – certainly a lot better than high school – so a trip to a campus can be a real motivator. It can be just the thing that finally gets your child to take an interest in the whole process. It also makes some students realize that maybe they should buckle down a bit and work a little harder on grades.

We took Molly to the University of North Carolina early in her junior year. She attended an information session there and heard how competitive the school is. It was a no–nonsense presentation that really opened her eyes. Suddenly, she realized that grades *did* count for something. She came back to high school a changed student – much more motivated and much more serious about her studies.

Planning the trip

You should allow at least a half day for a college visit. And don't try to jam too many into a weekend. Like visiting European churches, there's a saturation point; after a while the details start to blur, and you forget whether it was Cornell that had the really neat student union, or was it Ithaca that had sinks in the dorm rooms?

Before you plan a visit, write or call the admissions department. (The address and phone number are right there on your grid.) They are really helpful. They'll give you the schedule of information sessions and tours. They'll send you maps and parking permits. They'll send you a list of accommodations and restaurants in the area. Many schools will ask you to make an appointment for a particular information session or tour; others will say just stop by.

Information sessions sound deadly but they can be very helpful. These are large group sessions in which an admissions officer gives students and parents an overview of the school and the admission requirements: everything from overall costs and standardized test requirements to subject majors and football games. You'll pick up lots of information about the school and also all kinds of general information that will come in handy no matter what school your child is applying to. You can also get specific questions answered.

Most colleges offer guided tours. These take up to an hour and are usually run by students. (A cute tour guide will definitely help. If your child complains that the guide is a nerd, just remind him or her that the guides are not necessarily representative of the entire student body.) Campus tours hit the highlights – library, student union, a classroom building, etc. They're not essential, but one good reason to take the tour is it usually gets you into a dorm room, which is difficult to do on your own. Also, it gives you a chance to talk to the student tour guide, who can answer the types of questions you may not have had a chance to ask during the information session: Are vegetarian meals available? How many kids commute? How's the dorm food? etc.

Hang out for a while

Definitely allow some time for wandering around by yourselves. The student union is a crucial stop on any college visit. Not only is it the most happening place on campus – fast food, lounges, game rooms, fireplaces, cafes, etc. – but it also can provide a wealth of information about campus life. Check out the bulletin boards for notices about concerts, club meetings, poetry readings, rallies, and protests. Look at the ride board, where students who need a ride somewhere try to match up with students who have cars and are going in the same direction.

On a trip to Bucknell, we saw professors sitting in the cafeteria with students, engaged in animated conversation. That says something about the accessibility of faculty and the relationship between students and professors.

Spend as much time as possible in the student union. Sit for a while and just observe the interaction. Is the atmosphere boisterous or studious? Are kids keeping to themselves or calling across the room to each other? Try to visualize your son or daughter in these surroundings; you can bet your child will be doing the same thing. (One word of warning: student unions are empty on Sunday mornings.)

Go to the bookstore, and be prepared to spend some money. When we went to college, bookstores sold books. Today they're virtual department stores. Books are relegated to a separate area or floor, and the rest of the bookstore is stocked with sweatshirts and other clothing, school and computer supplies, souvenirs, CDs, candy, food items, etc. Most kids won't be able to resist buying a T–shirt or a mug with the school logo.

Check out the town (or the neighborhood if the college is in a big city). A Pizza Hut, Dunkin' Donuts or Taco Bell nearby will surely be a comforting sight to your child. (Except for Sophie, who has a real aversion to bean burritos. The sight of a Taco Bell two doors down from the dorm at the University of Michigan left a bad taste in her mouth. No pun intended.)

Molly was in her hippie phase when she visited North Carolina, and all the bead and crystal shops in Chapel Hill definitely made her feel more positive about the school. Carrie liked the thrift shops, bars, and village atmosphere of Cleveland Circle near Boston College.

Hopefully, you'll have good weather for the college visit. After Mike and his parents slogged through a muddy University of Massachusetts campus, the rest of the visit was a total washout. It's hard not to let bad weather affect your feelings about a place.

In any case, don't overdo it, and don't push it. If your kids don't like what they see, and if they just don't want to be there any more, give up. They'll definitely let you know when it's time to go, so just take your cues from them.

Kids generally like the first campus they visit, because just about any college campus looks a lot better than high school. When we took Katie and Coleen on their first college visit, to the University of Delaware, they both swore they would become Blue Hens. As the visits continue, the kids become somewhat jaded, but they also become more discriminating. They know what to look for; they know what they're comparing. They actually start to put all this stuff into perspective.

Remember, *you* may be reacting to the number of volumes in the library or the architectural integrity of the campus. *Your kid* will be reacting to what the students look like, how "pretty" the campus is, what the action is like on fraternity row, and how big the dorm rooms are.

Staying overnight

If you're staying overnight, even the motel or hotel you stay at can affect your child's feelings about the school. The University

Finding out about colleges

What's important to you ...

How safe is the campus?

How much does the meal plan cost?

How many meals per week are available?

Does the college offer financial aid?

How many volumes are in the library?

What are the graduation requirements?

What are the professors like?

Are the dorms locked at night?

Are freshmen allowed to have cars?

... What's important to your kid

What's the party scene like?

How far to a Pizza Hut?

What's the *very latest* that breakfast is served?

Where's the cash machine?

Can you have kegs in the dorms?

Where's the nearest mall?

What are the kids like?

Are the dorms co-ed?

Are freshmen allowed to have cars?

of Wisconsin dropped way down after we stayed at a seedy hotel that served the breakfast buffet on a radiator in the shabby lobby.

Sophie spent a sleepless night in Bloomington before we set out for the Indiana University campus. On the hotel's guest questionnaire, she left this note for the maid: "I know it's John Cougar's home state, but Indiana's not turning me on. Let's bolt." But the Mother Bear's pizza that night helped turn the tide a bit.

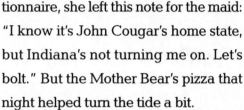

These kids all look like nerds. Can we get out of here?

Some schools rent rooms in the student union or in other buildings on campus. The rates are usually lower than at hotels, and you'll certainly get a feel for the atmosphere.

Expect weird kid reactions

Your child will like or dislike a campus for the strangest reasons. Molly fell in love with the University of Michigan because of the student protests going on in "the diag"that day. Sophie turned against the University of Delaware because there were "too many students" there (!!!!). College of William and Mary? – "too colonial." Penn State? – "too all-American." A trip to Indiana University was nearly ruined for us because we arrived there the same evening as a clog dancing exhibition. It was dusk as we walked from our car to one of the buildings, and we suddenly noticed, from everywhere, couples arriving for the exhibition. The women were in hoop skirts with crinolines and the men sported string ties. And this after spending the plane trip out trying to tell Sophie that Indiana was not filled with hayseeds.

Can I buy this sweatshirt? It's only 65 bucks!

The best story we ever heard is of a girl whose parents drove her three hours to Union College, but she wouldn't get out of the car because she didn't like the kind of shoes the students were wearing. She could not, she said, even consider a college with students who wore those shoes. There are lots of other reasons kids don't get out of the car: "school too small," "school too hilly," "kids too preppy," "kids carrying too many books." Expect anything.

Try to be neutral about your own feelings during these trips. Gushing about a particular school can be the kiss of death. We once asked Katie what exactly she had against a particular school, and she said, "Nothing, except for the fact that you like it so much."

Stay calm

One of your most important jobs on the college visit is to try to balance your child's reactions. It may be raining today, but it doesn't always rain here. Not everyone in Indiana clog dances. You're right, that kid is a nerd, but there are 35,000 kids here, and they're not all nerds. That kind of observation helps keep things in perspective.

Of course, one sure way to make the college trip more enjoyable for your child is to take a friend along—their friend, not yours! (But you already knew that.)

Sometimes, things work out best if you send your child on the college trip with a friend or with a friend's parents. We took Katie all over looking at colleges, and nothing turned her on. Then she went to Rutgers with a friend – we stayed home – and she fell in love with the place. Coincidence? Maybe. You know your child best, and if you think they'll do better without you, then encourage them to make other arrangements. They may know someone from their high school or have another friend who is already at a particular college. High school alumni are usually happy to show prospective students around "their" campus. Staying overnight on campus with the friend can give your child a great insider's view of the place.

So, things to remember:

• Keep it fun.
• Don't overstay your child's endurance.
• Drop some bucks in the bookstore.
• See a dorm room.
• Try to remain neutral.

The college trip is as important for the parent as for the prospective student. After all, you need to feel comfortable with the school also. And besides, it may very well be the last extended time you spend with your child.

But let's not get maudlin. There's still a lot of work to do.

SAT / ACT

ost colleges require applicants to take
standardized tests as part of the admissions process. The tests used
most often are the Scholastic Assessment Test (SAT) or, in some
parts of the country, the American College Testing program test
(ACT).

About the SATs

The SAT is the test required by most colleges, so let's focus
on that one first.

Administered by the College Board Testing Program of the
Educational Testing Service (ETS) in Princeton, New Jersey, SATs
are supposed to measure how well a student will do in college. They
have been surrounded by a great deal of controversy in recent years:

*T*he SATs are important, but they're not **all** important. (When's the last time a prospective employer asked for your SAT scores?) They're one of several measures that a college uses as a basis for admission.

How well do they really predict a student's success in college? Are they biased against females and minorities? How important should they be in determining admission to college?

ETS recently revised the SAT, the first change in the test since 1974. The new tests were first used in the spring of 1994. ETS says the test now requires more critical thinking and discourages guess work, and they have changed the name of the test from Scholastic *Aptitude* Test to Scholastic *Assessment* Test. The SAT is now referred to as SAT–I: Reasoning Test, and the Achievements as SAT–II: Subject Tests. We'll talk more about the details of the new SATs later in this chapter.

Most schools say that the standardized test scores are just one of several factors that they use in determining a student's likelihood of admission. Most important, schools say, is how well the student has done in high school – grades, class rank, and rigorousness of course selection, including honors and advanced placement courses, if available. Test scores are probably the next most important factor, except at a handful of schools that do not require or consider them.

(By the way, another reason to encourage your child to take advanced placement courses is that these courses can translate into college credit if an acceptable score is achieved on the AP test. Thanks to AP credits, some kids manage to graduate from college a semester early. Think of all the money you'll save!)

Usually, the bigger the school, the more important the test score. That's because for those schools, which receive tens of thousands of applications, SAT / ACT scores provide a quick and convenient yardstick, an objective measure that helps them put the applications into appropriate piles. Smaller schools, which have the luxury of looking more closely at individual applications, won't be as likely to automatically discount an application just because the test scores are low.

What the test is like

Each SAT-I is divided into seven sections: three verbal, three mathematical, and one experimental section that may be either verbal or mathematical. The experimental section doesn't count toward the score; it is used by ETS to test various new questions. However, the experimental section isn't marked in any way, so it's virtually impossible for students to know which section is experimental. The old Test of Standard Written English (TSWE), which was supposed to measure a student's language ability, has been dropped from the new version, largely because most colleges ignored it anyway.

Scores on the SATs range from a low of 200 to a high of 800 for the verbal and mathematical sections, respectively. So a perfect combined score would be 1600. Keep in mind that the national average SAT verbal score for 1993 was 424, and the average mathematical score was 478.

Recently, however, ETS made an important change in how it scores the SAT. It "recentered" the scoring scale, raising the average verbal score by 80 points and the average math score by 20 points. The new scoring system, first used for tests administered in the spring of 1995, was implemented, ETS says, so that average scores will fall around 1,000—500 for verbal and 500 for math. Sounds like a nice gift to students, but obviously colleges know about the adjustment and will, of course, adjust their standards accordingly.

Registering for the SATs

There is a lot of material out there about the SATs and how to prepare to take them. That's your child's job. Your job is to make certain that you both understand the SAT process: the dates, registration deadlines, fees, etc. Because the SATs are administered only on certain dates, you need to plan for them carefully.

Each year, ETS puts out a free bulletin and registration form, which gives test dates and sites, registration deadlines, and fees. This bulletin can be obtained from the high school guidance office. Make sure you see it early in your child's junior year so you and your child can plan the best date or dates to take the test. You must register for these dates well in advance – the bulletin gives the deadlines for each test. If you register late, you're subject to a late fee on top of the regular fee. If you're really late, you can't register at all, and may have to go to the test site as a stand-by.

The SAT is usually given on seven different dates throughout the year, typically in October, November, December, January, April, May, and June. Many students take the SAT once or twice in the spring of their junior year and then again in the fall of their senior year. (Many students have already taken the Preliminary Scholastic Assessment Test, or PSAT, in the fall of their junior year, or sometimes earlier. This is an abbreviated version of the SAT, taken as practice. The PSAT is also used to qualify for the National Merit Scholarship program.)

SATs are administered at selected high schools; not every high school is a test site. Many students feel more comfortable taking the SATs at their own high school or at one close by so they don't have to cope with a strange environment. Registering early means a better chance that your child will be able to take the test at his or her preferred location.

The first time your child registers for the SAT, he or she must do so by mail. If your child registers again, for another test date, he or she can do so by phone. The bulletin explains how. The mail form is somewhat tedious to fill out – No. 2 pencil only, fill in the boxes, etc. – especially if the student fills out the optional Student Descriptive Questionnaire (SDQ) that deals with the student's extracurricular activities, interests, and plans. If your child does fill out that part – and it's not really essential – it should be filled out only once. If and when the student registers for future SATs, he or she doesn't have to fill that part out again, because it's already on file. This report gets sent along to colleges with the scores, and it also goes to your child and your child's high school.

Reregistering by phone is quicker and easier, but it costs a little more money.

Whether your child registers by mail or by phone, he or she will receive an admission ticket in the mail. Check the ticket right away to make sure all the information is accurate. If not, you must immediately return the correction form included. Put the ticket in a safe place, and don't forget to have your child bring it to the test.

ETS offers lots of options about the SATs that are all explained in the registration bulletin and that all cost extra – these include changing a test date or location, getting a copy of the questions and correct answers, rushing the score report, etc. The less organized you are, the more it will cost you, because every time you need to change something, there's an extra fee.

When your child fills out the registration form, he or she can indicate which colleges should receive the scores. You get three for free; there's a fee for each additional score report. If you know which colleges your child plans to apply to, it's a good idea to send the scores at this time, rather than paying for them later. Don't worry if your child hasn't yet sent an application to the school. When the college gets the score report from ETS, it immediately starts a file on your child and will also start to send information to him or her. When the application comes in, the college will file it with the SAT score report.

Colleges must receive *official* score reports from ETS. Even though there is a place on most applications for the high school guidance office to fill in the SAT scores, the application will not be considered complete unless the score report is received directly from ETS.

When the test results are mailed to your child, the notification form will list which colleges have been sent the scores, as you indicated. It's a good idea to check off on your grid which colleges were sent the scores. This stuff gets very confusing, so use your grid and stay organized. You think you'll remember what you've done, but you won't, unless you mark it down and file it appropriately.

I'm not gonna sweat the SATs. **Really.** I'm not.

Preparing for the SATs

You now know the logistics of the SATs. So how can you help your child pre-

pare for them? The first thing to remember is that your child is probably extremely nervous about the entire prospect of taking the SATs.
That's because, no matter what colleges and high school guidance
counselors may say (and they virtually all say that the high school
record is the most important factor for admission), many students
still feel that their admission to the col-
lege of their choice hinges largely on

how well they score on the SATs. So don't
make matters worse by harping on the
SATs. The best thing you can do is try to
help your child gain some perspective
about the SATs in the scope of the rest of
his or her life. Keep your sense of humor
and balance about it and chances are
your child will also.

While ETS says there is no real
way to prepare for the SATs, because
they are supposed to measure aptitude,
not knowledge, there are many compa-
nies and individuals out there offering SAT preparation courses.
Most of them are quite expensive. Whether you encourage your
child to enroll in such a course depends on a lot of different factors,
including your child's motivation and your financial ability. Some
kids improve their scores by taking these courses, others don't. Take
your cue from your kid. If he or she wants to take a preparation
course – and you can afford it – then why not? Forcing someone
to take the course will probably backfire. The courses aren't magic.

They all require quite a bit of work on the part of the student. If
nothing else, these courses will give your child an opportunity to
take practice tests, get used to the types
of questions asked, and work out some of
their anxiety before the real thing comes
along.

Where did you
put that ticket
for the SATs?

Probably the best-known of the
SAT preparation courses is Princeton
Review, which claims to raise students'
SAT scores by an average of 110 to 160
points. They use young, "with it" instruc-
tors who talk to the kids on their own level.
Their basic philosophy is that the SAT
doesn't measure anything except how
well a person takes the SAT. What
Princeton Review does, mostly, is help the kids "psych out" the test.
Yes, they employ some gimmicks, but they also do a lot of vocabulary and math review, which doesn't hurt. Princeton Review also
has available a computer version of their review course.

One of the best things about many of the SAT preparation
courses is that they offer a free preview class for parents and students that is really a condensed version of the course. Go to it with
your child. You'll both be able to get a sense of whether the course
will work for your child.

If you think your child will respond better in a one-on-one
situation, you might consider hiring a private tutor for individual-
ized instruction. This can be especially helpful if your child needs

to brush up in a very specific area. Ask around and get recommendations from other parents. Some high school teachers tutor in the evening, and they are generally less expensive than formal tutoring services.

There are other alternatives as well. Some high schools offer free or low-cost courses on SAT preparation. Also, there are many books and computer software packages available that help prepare students for the SATs. ETS puts out books that have *actual* tests and answers in them. Other books have practice tests that are *similar* to actual SATs.

I know if I take it just one more time I can crack 1200.

Try to encourage your child to do some preparation for the SATs, even if it's just taking a few practice tests at home. That way he or she will at least know what to expect.

When to take the SATs, and how often

How many times should your child take the SATs? That depends. For some, once is enough. Guidance counselors advise that if you score better than 1200 combined, don't take them again. But if your kid is one of those perfectionists who always think they can do better, then there's probably no stopping them. There's no limit to the number of times you can take the SAT, but remember this: *Each time your child takes the test, the score is entered on his or her record.*

Every time you send a score report to a college, the scores from all past tests appear on the report.

The only time a score won't go on your child's record and be reported is if he or she takes the test and then cancels the scores by filling out a special application form and sending it to ETS within a specified number of days. Some students do this on purpose, during their sophomore year, just to get used to the test.

Some schools say they will take the highest scores from one single test administration; others say they will take the highest verbal and highest math, even if taken on different dates. The thinking here is that students can have a bad day and score *lower* than their real ability; but it's unlikely that students can score *higher* than their true level. But do remember that colleges will see all the scores from each time the test was taken, unless the scores have been canceled.

A reasonable scenario is to take the SATs in April or June of the junior year, and, if necessary, again in November of the senior year. If your child is taking an SAT preparation course, TAKE IT RIGHT BEFORE HE OR SHE TAKES THE TEST FOR THE FIRST TIME. That way your child will get the advantage of the course the first time out. By spacing the tests at least two months apart, your child will have a chance to receive the results and do any additional necessary preparation before taking the test again. Taking the test in the junior year also means your child will have the scores in time to complete any applications to schools with rolling admissions or early decision options. And if the scores are good, they won't have to be bothered taking them again in senior year, which is a definite plus.

SAT-II: Subject tests

Now a word about the Subject Tests, or SAT–II. These are also administered by ETS, and everything we've said about the SATs in terms of dates, deadlines, fees, and the need to be organized applies to the SAT-II as well. These tests are offered on the same dates as the SAT-I. But you can't take the SAT-I and the SAT-II on the same day. You can take either one, two or three Subject Tests on any one date.

The SAT-IIs are one-hour tests that are supposed to measure a student's knowledge of various subject areas – English composition, literature, math, biology, French, American history, etc. They are scored the same way as the SAT-I, on a 200–800 scale, but where the SAT-I is supposed to measure aptitude, the SAT-IIs are supposed to measure what you have actually learned in a particular subject. Therefore, it's a good idea to take the SAT-II as close to completion of the particular subject as possible. For instance, many high schools offer an advanced biology course during sophomore year. If that's a good subject for your child, he or she should definitely take the Biology Subject Test at the end of that school year.

The most selective schools require three SAT-IIs. Other schools want only the English Composition test. Still others don't require any SAT-IIs, but of course they will look at the scores if they're sent. So if your child has a good probability of doing well on a particular test, it's a smart idea to take it, even though it may not be required. Here again, your child's scores on the SAT-II become a permanent part of the score report, and they go along to any school that's sent a report.

Recent changes in the SATs

I hate that reading comprehension. And now there's even more.

ETS says their new SATs, which were rolled out in March 1994, will force students to do more critical thinking and less guesswork. Critics of ETS say, yes, the new SATs are a step in the right direction, but a baby step at best.

Here are some of the changes:

• Students are permitted to use calculators to solve math problems.

• Ten of the 60 math questions require students to solve problems and produce their own answers on a grid, rather than choosing from multiple choice responses.

• A greater percentage of the verbal section is now reading comprehension.

• The antonym questions in the verbal section have been eliminated. These were the questions that asked "What is the opposite of funny?" and gave five multiple choice responses from which to choose.

That's about it. ETS says that in nationwide trials of the new tests, scores did not differ significantly from the old versions. Remember, though, that in 1995 ETS "padded" the SAT scores. So scores before and after that year aren't really comparable.

A word about ACT

In some parts of the country, including the Midwest and South, students are more likely to take the ACT (American College Testing) program. Unlike the SAT, the ACT is divided into four parts—English, math, reading (which includes literature, science, and social studies), and science reasoning. The ACT is more like the SAT-I and SAT-II rolled into one, testing subject knowledge as well as aptitude. The ACT is scored on a 1 to 36 scale, with the national average at 20.6.

Registration and test procedures are similar to the SAT. For specific information, write to ACT Registration, PO Box 414, Iowa City, IA 52243–0414.

Although the SAT is still considered the "gold standard," an increasing number of schools will accept the ACT in its place.

Standardized tests are a rite of passage your college-bound youngster must go through, like driving tests and first dates. Just try to remember that your child is sweating these tests even more than you are. After all, *you* don't have to sit in that hot room with your number two pencils and the big clock on the wall. So do all you can to help them get through it.

The Application

*N*ow it's time to work on the application packet. By application packet, we mean all the components your child will be sending to the college: the student's part of the application form, the guidance part, the essay, the letters of recommendation, and any other supporting material. Since many colleges, especially the larger ones, do not offer interviews, the colleges don't actually see or get to talk to any applicants. So the application packet is all they have to go on to make a decision about your child. That's why it's so important.

Of course, the completed application form must be accurate and neat, and it must be submitted on time. (The deadlines

*F*illing out the application takes time and effort. Don't rush through it. Each application is different. By the sixth one, you'll probably start to get the hang of it.

should be on your grid.) Keith tells a story that he spilled coffee on his Columbia University application, blotted it dry to a nice tan stain, sent it in, and got accepted anyway, but we would not advise your child to take that chance.

While the application is of course primarily the student's responsibility, there are lots of things a parent can do to help. Be sensitive to your child's needs. If he or she wants to do it all alone, that's great. If you happen to have that kind of child (lucky you), then your role may be nothing more than proofreading the final copy and signing the check for the application fee. But most kids want and need a little help, whether in the form of someone to type the application or just to discuss its contents. In any case, try to make yourself available when your child finally decides to tackle the application.

Some schools have a two-part application. Part I includes only the basics. After you send Part I back with the application fee, the college sends Part II, which is much more detailed. Most colleges, however, send everything at once.

Applications vary in their format and degree of complexity. The University of Massachusetts, a large state school that mainly goes by the numbers (standardized test scores and class rank), has a relatively simple and straightforward application form. Plug in the names and the numbers and you're set. Cornell, an Ivy League school, has a more demanding application that asks for essays and brief responses to individual questions.

A growing number of colleges across the country (including Harvard, New York University, Swarthmore, Williams, Bucknell, and other mostly small, private schools) now accept a "common application" as well as their own. These schools encourage the use of the common application and do not make any distinction between it and their own application form.

Obtain a copy of the common application from the guidance office. The schools that accept it are listed right on the application. If your child's schools are listed, it will make life a lot easier for both of you.

You should approach all applications in the same way: each should be filled out carefully, neatly, and with attention to detail. Allow enough time. If your child tries to fill out even the simplest application on the run, in a few minutes before basketball practice or while waiting to get picked up for the movies, it will probably lead to mistakes.

What to do

Advance preparation is crucial. Here's how to proceed:

• First, you and your child should read through the applications as they come in, to get familiar with the information needed.

• Now, make several copies of each blank application, and then keep the original applications in a safe place. *It's absolutely essential for your child to work on a copy of the application before doing the final one.*

• Next, have your child prepare a sheet of vital statistics that lists this information:

> *student's social security number*
> *high school code*
> *dates of attendance at high school*
> *senior year courses*
> *extracurricular activities*
> *dates and scores on standardized tests*
> *summer jobs and activities*
> *parents' education*

This information is needed on virtually *all* applications, and it will be a lot easier if you have this sheet handy for your reference.

• Prepare a typed résumé listing your child's extracurricular activities, awards and honors, and employment and volunteer experience. Keep it to one page and put your child's name and social security number at the top. Some colleges give applicants the option of including this résumé as a separate insert instead of cramming the information into the alloted space on the application. When you do this, type "see attached" in the appropriate place on the application. Here is a sample résumé.

Sample Résumé

Name
Social Security Number

High School Activities

Varsity softball	9, 10, 11, 12 (Captain)
Principal's Advisory Committee	10, 11, 12
Ridellion (school newspaper)	10, 11, 12
Projections (school literary magazine)	10
Student Government Organization	9
Environmental Action Club	10
Students Against Drunk Driving	10, 11, 12
Latin Club	12
Dinner Dance Committee	9
Field Hockey	9
Statistician for girls' varsity basketball team	9, 10, 11
Ski Club	9, 10, 11, 12

Awards and Honors

New Jersey Bar Association Bill of Rights Competition—Third Place
Chosen for the Gifted and Talented Program
Girls' State—Selected as alternate
Career Institute—Selected as alternate
Honor Roll
First Team All League, Pitcher—BCSL American Softball League, 1989–1991
Honorable Mention All County, Pitcher—All Bergen County Softball, 1989–1991

Community, Work, and Summer Activities

Volunteer at Cherry Hill Elementary School After-School Program, 1988
River Edge Recreation camp counselor, 1987–1992
Softball umpire for River Edge Girls Athletic League, 1989
Salesperson at O'Shea's Sporting Goods, River Edge, 1990–1991
Summer softball (UGALS and Metropolitan Girls Softball League), 1985–1991
Attended University of Michigan Softball Pitching Camp, 1989

Most applications request that you use a typewriter to complete them. Some will say "print neatly or type." At least one, from Penn State, says, "Fill out in either black or blue ink." This so threw one parent that he actually called the school and asked if it was okay to type the application. Actually, if you or your child has incredibly neat handwriting, it's probably all right to fill out the application by hand. (Keith, the one who spilled coffee on his Columbia application, has also never typed an application in his life, and he's now getting a Ph.D. at Johns Hopkins.) But if the handwriting is anything less than perfect, use a typewriter.

I can't believe I can't use the computer for these applications!

Some schools, recognizing the difficulty of typing an application, allow students to apply electronically, via a computer disc or by modem. New York University and the entire State University of New York (SUNY) system are among those joining the computer trend.

Unfortunately, most application forms are still set up for typewriters rather than computers. If your kid is like most, he or she is probably quite proficient on a computer, but the typewriter may be pretty alien territory. Remember, it is not cheating if you or someone else does the actual typing of the application, as long as the information is accurate. Try to get your hands on a good typewriter with automatic correction capability. You'll need it.

Now do it

Here's a good way to approach the application. Your child should fill out one of the copies, by hand, with or without your help. (If he or she has the sheet of vital statistics handy, it will be a lot easier.) Go over the draft with your child, and feel free to make suggestions. Then whoever is best with the typewriter should type the application. But start with a copy first. Many applications allow a specified amount of space for an answer, and you want to be sure that the answer fits in that space. Typing the application is a lot trickier than it looks. Practice on copies first. When you have a perfect copy, do the real thing. But always keep a blank copy. In case you really mess up the original, you can use the copy. (Or call the school and ask for another application.)

When the application form is completed, make sure the student reads it over carefully to check for any errors. Don't freak out if there is an error. The application is not a typing test; you are allowed to use White-out to make a correction. Just make sure the application isn't sloppy. If it is neat and readable, you're okay.

The rest of the packet

Some applications require one or more essays. Some ask for a specific topic or topics, others ask for a personal statement, or an essay on any topic of the student's choosing. Some colleges do not ask for an essay, or they say that it is optional. Even if the application does not request one, it's a good idea to include a personal statement anyway.

The essay is the single most difficult part of the application, and the reason applications sit around in desk drawers until the last minute. Don't worry. The next chapter will tell you exactly how to get your kid to write a decent essay.

Some applications ask for anywhere from one to three letters of recommendation, and they may specify who should write the letters: a teacher, someone who knows the student on a personal basis, an employer, etc. The application may include a form for the letter writer to use, or ask that the letter writer send his or her own letter. Seek these people out early, and allow the person enough time. Most colleges will ask that the letters be sent directly by the writer to the school. If that's the case, provide the writer with a stamped, addressed envelope. Make it as easy as possible. Let them know the date the letter is due. The person who writes the letter of recommendation may or may not share its contents with your child. Obviously, your child will want to ask for letters only from those people who will write a favorable recommendation. Other possible sources for these letters, besides teachers, are coaches, pastors, employers, and family friends. If the application doesn't ask for a letter of recommendation, include one in the application packet anyway. It sure can't hurt.

Also include in the application packet anything pertinent that will present the student in the best light. This may include, for instance, a copy of a special honor or award. But do not overdo it. No scrapbooks, no photographs, no videotapes, no ribbons or medals, unless specifically requested.

Don't forget to include the check for the application fee. (Application fees vary from $10 to $50 or more. This fee may be waived for families who cannot afford to pay it.) Include the student's social security number on the memo portion of the check. (Again, always include the student's social security number on any communication with the college. Your child's social security number will also be his or her ID number in most colleges.) Usually, you will be requested to staple the check to the application. (Be careful though: Boston University requests, in *very* small print, that *nothing* be stapled to the application.)

Many applications also include a postcard to fill out so the college can acknowledge receipt of the application. Do it! You'll both rest a lot easier once that postcard is returned.

When you've got it all together, make copies of everything: the application, the postcard, the check, the essay, the letters, etc. Put the copies in your folders. Should the application get lost, at least you'll have everything together and duplicating it won't be a problem. It's also a good idea to know exactly what you've sent to each college.

The application goes to guidance

Now comes the really scary part. You've got to give the application packet to guidance, and that means it's now out of your direct control. The guidance office always has a portion of the application to fill out, related to grades, class rank, etc., and in many cases the college asks that the entire packet go to guidance to be completed and sent in. Because students and parents sometimes encounter problems in dealing with guidance, we've devoted a whole separate chapter to it. See chapter 9.

But a few basic rules:

(1) Give the application to guidance as early as possible to avoid the last minute rush.

(2) Make sure you know what the guidance office is going to say about your child. In other words, verify the class rank, SAT scores, school activities, etc. ahead of time. Many high schools give seniors a personal profile form to fill out. The student should complete this form and add any other pertinent information that would be useful for the guidance department to know, since most applications have a place for a recommendation by guidance. Better yet, have the student get to know the guidance counselor in advance, during sophomore year. Encourage your child to show his or her face so that the counselor will know the student personally rather than just as a name and a class rank.

(3) Write a detailed note for the guidance counselor listing what he or she has to do to complete that part of the application packet. While many guidance counselors are quite competent, others may not be, so the more help you give them, the better.

(4) If you really want to be helpful, take the packet to the post office before giving it to guidance, have it weighed, and put the appropriate postage on it.

(5) Have your child bug the guidance office on a daily basis to make sure the application has been sent out.

The idea here is to keep tabs on guidance. Check on whatever you can. Verify their information all along the way. *Your* guidance office may know what it's doing, but don't assume that's always the case.

If, like most, your child is sending in an average of six or seven applications, this process will be long, time-consuming, nerve-wracking, and grueling. But it does get a little easier with each application.

The best feeling in the world is when that last application is in the mail, or even better, when that last postcard is back and you know that all the colleges have received the applications.

But wait a minute. We've still got to deal with the essay.

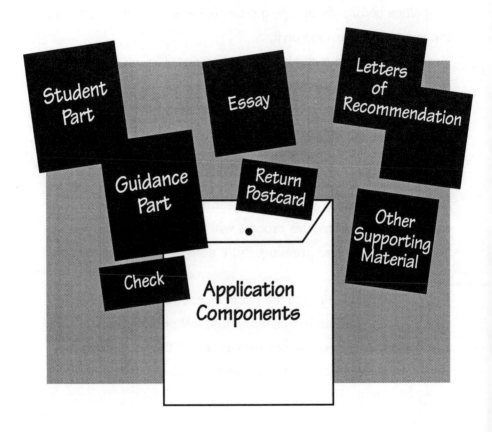

Student Part

Essay

Letters of Recommendation

Guidance Part

Return Postcard

Other Supporting Material

Check

Application Components

The Essay

h my God! The essay. We've arrived at that awful moment of truth. The application is neatly typed; it's all ready to go to the guidance office and into the mail except for one small problem: your kid has to write an essay, and that seems to be a monumental stumbling block.

Many college applications require an essay. Some suggest one. Others don't mention an essay. It's always a good idea to include one anyway, with the hope of enhancing the application.

Some colleges ask for an essay on a specific topic. It could be a book or a person that's had an influence on the student's life; why your child is choosing this particular college; a world event that

*I*t's time for the dreaded essay, but don't sweat it. Here are some tips to help you help your child overcome this barrier and turn out an essay that will enhance the application.

moved the student deeply. Other schools ask applicants to submit a brief (one page) personal statement. "What do you want us to know about you?" they ask. It's a chance for your child to tell the school something about himself or herself, something that may not come through on questions 1 through 25 of the application form.

The problem is, if your kid is like most, he or she will not want to write the essay; in fact, your child will probably dread the essay and keep putting it off. Can you blame them? Writing doesn't come easily to most people, and your child will probably feel that no matter what he or she writes, it won't be good enough.

Remember, the biggest reason the essay is included is so that the school can see how well the applicant can use the English language – spelling, punctuation, vocabulary, etc. Second, the school is trying to get a feel for what distinguishes this applicant from thousands of others. It helps them see the person behind all the numbers. Don't put too much stock in the essay. An outstanding essay won't compensate for a lousy class rank and low test scores, but it just may make a difference in the case of a borderline application.

Some students solve the essay problem by having other people, usually their parents, write the essay for them. This isn't a good idea for all the obvious reasons – ethics, morality, etc. But it's also not a good idea because it's not very difficult to spot an essay written by a forty-five-year-old professional. So, for a number of reasons, you won't be doing your child a favor if you actually write the essay for him or her.

Some schools ask for a copy of a paper that was graded by the applicant's teacher – just to make sure the student actually wrote it.

But most schools are pretty flexible about the essay, and there are many ways a parent can help. If you know your child can write the essay but is just too lazy, scared, or unmotivated, try some gentle prodding. But remember, a gentle reminder to you may be unbearable nagging to your child. One tactic is to set a deadline, maybe a month away, for a first draft. It may be a good idea to suggest that a first draft of the essay be written by Labor Day before senior year. Never mind if you don't have the applications yet. Just work toward a draft of the personal statement. Your child will probably need it for at least some of the applications, and it can also be adapted for those applications that require other types of responses. At the very least, it will show your kid that yes, he or she can indeed write an essay.

If your child still isn't writing the essay, find out why. Most kids will say they don't know what to write about. Tell them they can write about anything: career plans, a favorite subject in school, a sport, a hobby, a trip or vacation, an opinion they have about anything, their goals, their dreams, their regrets, their past, their future, their family, their sister or brother, a friend, an accident, an illness, an award, a summer job, a book, a movie, ANYTHING. Or it can be a piece of creative writing – a (very) short story or a poem.

Anything that helps to differentiate the applicant is usually good, within limits. One student applying to Wesleyan was asked to write an essay in his own hand. He drew an outline of his hand and wrote the essay in it. (He was accepted.) Don't be too cute, however. There is a fine line between creative and weird or annoying. Help your child use his or her best judgment.

Here's one approach to helping your child write the essay. Sit down at the kitchen table with your child and try to find a topic from the above list. Then ask him or her lots of questions; interview your child. Take notes. Tell your child to look over the notes and try to organize them into an essay.

There are books of sample essays which may help your child get started. Or try to get hold of essays written by other kids in past years. The idea here is not to copy but to help your child get an idea of what's expected and what is acceptable.

Tell your child to just start writing and not to worry about what he or she is saying. Assure your child that it's probably going to be a lot better than he or she thinks. The important thing is to get something – *anything* – down on paper.

If your kid is really hung up about writing, tell him or her to make believe they're talking to a friend. Write down what they say, use a tape recorder, or tell them to make believe they're writing a letter to a friend.

TELL THEM TO JUST DO IT ALREADY. When we gave Katie a deadline and it came and went, and all our nagging was for naught, we finally got really tough. She woke up one Saturday morning and we told her that after breakfast she had to go back to her room and she couldn't leave until she wrote her essay. It worked.

Sophie also procrastinated. We tried the same thing. She sat in her room all day talking on the phone and reading. We asked her what we had to do to get her to write the essay. She said pay her. So we did! We settled on $20 for a first draft.

These are extreme examples, but we're talking about kids who really could write but for whatever reason refused to do so. Most kids want to write an essay but have real trouble getting started. Just let them know that you're going to help them. No, you won't write the essay for them, but yes, you will help them select a topic and organize their thoughts.

Princeton Review suggests that students put their first draft under their pillow for a week or so, and then look at it again. They will probably be pleasantly surprised. Most likely it won't need much work. Let them fix it up, carefully read it for spelling and other errors, and then show it to you. If you're not sure about it, find someone with editing skills who can help. Often teachers are more than willing to review their students' college essays and make suggestions and editing corrections. There's one teacher like that in every high school; make sure your kid finds that teacher.

DON'T BE TOO CRITICAL. Remember, no college is expecting a Hemingway-quality essay. But the college *is* expecting a neat manuscript, with no spelling or punctuation errors. If you find any errors, point them out. That's not really cheating, and if it is, everyone does it, and the colleges know that. Just make sure that the essay is your child's and not yours.

A few words about mechanics. Have your child put his name and social security number at the top of the page, just in case the essay gets separated from the rest of the application packet. Try to personalize the essay for each college. "That's why I want to go to Princeton..." "What I'd like Penn State to know about me is...." This is real easy to do if you have a computer.

Be brief – no more than one single-spaced page. Make sure everything is spelled correctly. Be neat. Use good quality paper.

Remember, writing an essay, like any other task, will be a lot easier for your child if he or she gets some encouragement, knows you're there to help, and also knows you won't tear apart the end product.

You won't believe how good you'll both feel when the essay is finally written.

Dealing With Guidance Counselors

*D*epending on the high school guidance office to adequately shepherd your child through the college admissions process is like counting on your doctor to restore you to good health after a serious illness. Sure, they play an important role. But remember: they've got lots of students (patients) to worry about; they don't know everything; they have been known to make mistakes;

*M*ake friends with the high school guidance department, but don't depend on them to steer your child through the process. That's your job.

and they're not always receptive to lots of questions and "outside interference." When you're sick, it's your body, and no one knows it or cares about it as much as you do; and when your child is embarking on the college admissions process, it's the students and the parents who have the most interest in the outcome.

The truth is, guidance counselors vary tremendously in their competence. Some are incredibly well informed and take a real interest in each child they see. Others are not as good. Stories about experiences with guidance – good and bad – abound. So the lesson to be learned is that you must get and stay involved. Utilize their help and resources, but don't abdicate your responsibility to the guidance office.

As one Ivy League admissions officer commented,

high school guidance offices are the weak link in the college admissions process. They don't know as much as they should, they don't keep up with new information and trends, and they certainly don't know as much as they should about their own students.

Sadly, the guidance office can be seriously misinformed or out-of-date. In recent years schools that have rolling admissions policies – that means they accept and process applications on a continuous basis – have become more numerous. But too often guidance counselors are stuck in a time warp, still operating as though January and Feburary are the only important deadlines. Obviously, you will have the best and most up-to-date information about the handful of colleges your child is applying to. Make sure the guidance office knows at least what you know about those schools.

With a little concentrated effort, you can learn as much about the college admissions process as the average high school guidance counselor. So don't depend on the guidance office to do it all. Get to know them. Utilize them. Work with them. Pick their brains, of course. But don't take what they say as gospel. And when it comes to things that you are truly dependent on guidance for – things like filling out certain parts of the application and sending it in on time – talk to them. Remind them. Keep looking over their shoulder. Haunt them.

Of course, guidance counselors can and often do play a very helpful role. At their best, guidance counselors have a wealth of knowledge about colleges and can bring this to bear in helping your child make selections and complete the application process.

The problem is, in many cases, they just don't know each student well enough to make a good match. Here's how you can help.

Help guidance to help your child

First, encourage your child, early on in high school, to get to know his or her guidance counselor. Yes, that can be a drag, but it will definitely pay off when college application time rolls around. It's never too early for high school students to drop by the guidance office and start discussing college plans. The better the guidance counselor knows the student, the more he or she will be able to help, the better the recommendation will be, and the less likelihood that there will be an error. Some guidance offices provide students with a form to fill out, listing the student's extracurricular activities, interests, work experience, etc. These are the kinds of things guidance needs to know, not only to help your child select possible schools, but also to help the guidance counselors write a better, more personalized recommendation.

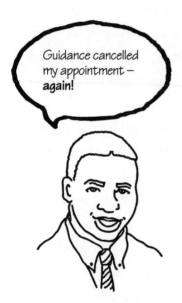

Guidance cancelled my appointment – **again!**

An article in the *New York Times* quoted college admissions officers who talked about how guidance offices were actually damaging students' chances of getting accepted to colleges. They told of guidance counselors who wrote form letters of recommendation for their students, often sending the same letter in for several students applying to the same school. The admissions officers said it was difficult for them not to react negatively to those applications.

Many high schools set up meetings between the guidance counselor and the parents. They're a good idea because, even though you've done your homework and feel that you know quite a bit, you may pick up some valuable information. For instance, Sophie had a long-time interest in ballet, and the guidance office suggested she apply to Indiana University because of its very strong program in the performing arts, a fact we had not known. Even if you don't get any really useful information, consider this meeting an important step in the process of getting the guidance office to know your child better.

Many guidance offices have a good collection of college brochures and videos; stop by and borrow them. They also usually have numerous college guides and other reference materials. Borrowing them can save you a lot of money.

If you want the guidance department to help you, you've got to help them. Have your child keep them informed about his or her college choices, and be considerate of the guidance department's work load. At all costs avoid the last-minute rush – usually Thanksgiving to Christmas. Make sure your child gets the applications in early, allowing the guidance counselor enough time to process them. (Be sure to note on your grid the date each application was delivered to guidance).

One problem that comes up frequently is that applications that come in early, during September, are often delayed because the class ranks, an essential piece of information required for the application, are not ready. This is both mind-boggling and frustrating. The guidance office will tell you that it can't compute class ranks until after summer school. Okay, summer school usually ends long before Labor Day, and calculating ranks should take a matter of hours, not days or weeks. Excuses will abound: the computer room flooded; the statistician has hepatitis. In one school recently, when the ranks finally did come in – late September – they had to be completely refigured after one student detected an error in his own rank.

On this issue of ranks, talk to guidance early, during your child's junior year. Tell them your child will be applying to schools with rolling or early admissions and you want to make sure that the calculation of ranks won't hold up the application. That at least will let them know someone will be watching and waiting. As soon as school starts, ask guidance about the ranks. Hound them as often as it takes. Keep the pressure on them. Better yet, round up some other parents whose children are also sending in applications early. Be firm, but don't lose your cool. Remember, you need guidance more than they need you.

Helpful hints in dealing with guidance

While it's true that guidance offices are very familiar with applications, you should still make things as easy as possible for them. A few suggestions:

• Take the application packet to the post office, have it weighed, and affix the appropriate postage. Better yet, ask guidance to give you back the packet so you can mail it yourself. The school may be reluctant to do this, because of the possibility that students will tamper with guidance's portion of the application. Tell them to seal that part up separately.

• Attach little yellow stickies to each part of the application that requires guidance to do something: "Sign here," "Fill in SAT scores here," "Enclose transcript," etc. Write a cover note with big bold type indicating the deadline, or just reminding them that this is a "rolling" application and it needs to go in ASAP. The cover note should also list all the components that need to be included in the packet: the application form, two recommendation letters, one essay, etc.

Guidance said they'll
send it out next week.
(Yeah, right.)

• Wait three days and then have your child stop in the guidance office to see if the application has been sent. If not, ask why. We heard about one high school guidance office that held up all applications going to a particular college so that they could all be sent in together. That's a disaster if the school is one with rolling admissions, where applications that are received earlier have an easier time.

Your child should stop in every other day until the application is in the mail. If there is a prolonged, unexplained delay, call the guidance office yourself and ask for an explanation. Be firm, but be nice, because, as we said, you need guidance more than they need you.

• Many applications require guidance to send in a mid-year report, detailing a student's grades at the end of the first semester of senior year. As soon as January exams are over, have your child remind the guidance counselor to send those reports in.

The more organized you are, the easier it will be to help the guidance office process your child's applications in a timely and organized manner.

You're almost there. Your child has filled out his or her applications, written the essay, gotten the letters of recommendation, and you know guidance has sent out the applications. You're almost home free. One more little bit of effort and you can just sit back and wait for the acceptances to roll in.

Applying for Financial Aid

few quick words:

• Applying for financial aid is a completely separate process from applying for admission to the college and cannot be completed until after January of the senior year.

• It requires an incredible level of financial detail – similar to the information provided on your federal income tax return.

• Standards to qualify for need-based scholarships or other grants are fairly stringent, but there are other sources of financial aid, including loans and work-study programs.

Although some colleges award grants based on academic merit or athletic ability, most financial aid is awarded on the

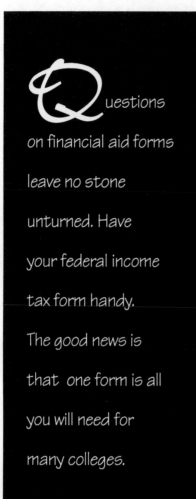

Questions on financial aid forms leave no stone unturned. Have your federal income tax form handy. The good news is that one form is all you will need for many colleges.

basis of need. Theoretically, most colleges make "need-blind" decisions about whether a student will be accepted. In other words, they say that they evaluate the student's application with no regard to the student's ability to pay. Once the student is admitted, they say, the college will work out a financial aid package to make sure he or she can afford to attend. (The college's idea of sufficient financial aid may be considerably different from your own. Realize that there might be room for negotiation, and don't hesitate to call the college and whine a little – it's worth a shot.) Privately, some admissions officers say that, given their colleges' own financial constraints, they may smile somewhat more favorably on an applicant who can pay his or her own way.

Nevertheless, the general thinking remains that if you need financial aid, you should apply for it.

The good news about the financial aid process is that you
fill out one common application, which is used by all the colleges.
(Some colleges may also have their own financial aid forms, in addition to the standard one.) The bad news is that the application is
very detailed and time-consuming to complete, and the requirements to receive financial aid are very stringent.

Sources of financial aid vary: state and federal governments,
the college itself, private foundations. Types of financial aid also
vary: outright grants, loans, and work-study programs. Financial
aid often comes in the form of a package that may include a com-
bination of the above, with an increasing emphasis on loans.

Financial aid forms

The form used by all colleges for all federal aid and for much
of the state aid available is the Free Application for Federal Student
Aid, or FAFSA. As the name implies, there is no charge for pro-
cessing this form. An additional form required by some schools is
the Financial Aid Form, or FAF, generated by the College Scholarship
Service (CSS) of the College Board. In addition, some schools also
require their own financial aid application.

These forms ask about a number of different factors: family income, savings and other assets, student's expected earnings,
family debt, number of other children in college, etc. Based on a
standard formula, the family's expected contribution is determined.

The difference between the cost of the college and the family contribution is the amount of aid for which you are eligible.

While the financial aid application is generic and the formula is consistent, individual colleges sometimes interpret the data differently. So the financial aid package you are given by one college may not be the same as that from another college.

This same application is also used to determine your eligibility for a variety of state and federal loans. Guidelines about these loans change from year to year, so even if you think you may not be eligible, it doesn't hurt to apply.

The FAFSA and other forms can be obtained from the high school guidance office or the college admissions office. The FAFSA cannot be filed until after January 1, and it requires information from the previous year, the same information you will need to file your federal income tax return. Deadlines for filing the FAFSA and other forms vary, but it's important to file them as soon as possible.

Even if you are not eligible for need-based aid, your child may receive aid based on academic merit or athletic ability. Check directly with each college to see what is available. For instance, some local alumni associations award grants based on academic achievement. That resulted in a $1500 grant for Molly. Carrie's softball talent made her an excellent candidate for an athletic scholarship.

Obtaining financial aid for college is an intricate process, and this chapter only skims the surface. Check bookstores and libraries, and call the colleges. Most have extremely helpful financial aid offices. Take the time to do some research, and it could pay off.

Following Up

ou should be feeling pretty good by now. All the applications are completed, and you know that the guidance office has sent them to the colleges. You also know that the test scores have been sent (you checked that off on your grid), and you have even followed up to make sure that any letters of recommendation have been sent. But your work is not *quite* over yet.

Remember those little postcards that you sent in with the applications, the ones that acknowledged receipt of the application? Well, keep on the lookout for them. They usually are returned within two to three weeks. *If you don't receive a card back, don't hesitate to call the school to make sure it has received the appli-*

*T*he applications, score reports, and letters of recommendation are all in.

You're feeling pretty good right now.

Just a few more tasks, and you're home free.

cation. Most schools will gladly give you this information over the telephone. As receipt of each application is acknowledged, don't forget to check it off on the grid. This is really important. Laurie applied to Rutgers College in New Jersey and never heard from them. After all of her friends had heard one way or the other, she called the school, only to find out it had never received her application and that it was too late to do anything about it.

Follow up with guidance to be sure they send in all required mid-year reports. These are necessary even if the school has already accepted the student.

As schools start reviewing applications, they will usually let you know if any particular piece of the application is missing, e.g., score reports, letters of recommendation. Follow up as soon as possible with any missing pieces.

If your child is notified by a college that he or she is deferred from early decision or placed on a waiting list, it doesn't hurt to encourage the child to call the school to get more feedback. When Jeff was deferred from early notification at Indiana University, he called and was told that if he made a B average on his first-quarter grades, he would probably be admitted. When Dave was rejected from the University of Colorado, it turned out that the school made the decision based on faulty information – a mix-up about two high schools with the same name. If he hadn't followed up and asked why he was rejected, the mistake might not have been discovered. He was, in fact, admitted.

Now, that doesn't mean that you or your child should call every school he or she is not accepted at; it does mean that if something doesn't sound right about the decision, it doesn't hurt to check it out.

Once your child is accepted

Now that the acceptances are rolling in, make sure you follow instructions carefully. Most schools give students a deadline of early May to let the school know if they will be attending. If your child definitely knows he or she will not be attending, notifying the school earlier may help another student get in. But don't hesitate to take all the time needed if your child is undecided; just don't blow the deadline. Many schools will go to great lengths to woo accepted students – calls from alumni, invitations to food-filled receptions near your home, even weekends at the college. Encourage your child to use these opportunities to learn as much as possible about the colleges.

Once your child is accepted at a school, the school will begin sending you important information. Read all of it carefully. Some require a deposit to hold a dorm room.

If your child is undecided at this point or wait-listed at his or her first choice, consider sending a deposit to more than one school just to be covered. These deposits are refundable, if the student does not attend the school. Again, you must apply for a refund on any of these deposits within a certain amount of time.

Read all the material carefully, do what you have to do to hold a place, and mark down any necessary deadlines.

If your child doesn't respond positively to a school by the deadline, the school will assume he or she is not going there and will offer the spot to someone else. So make sure your child lets the school know within the allowed time.

Wasn't It Fun?

Well, now it's all over and done with. You've survived the process, you've helped your child, and you've learned quite a bit.

Pack up your books, catalogs and videos, your file folders, the practice SAT/ACT exams, and the grid. *But don't throw anything out*, especially if you have another child about to embark on the process. True, a lot of this material becomes outdated fairly quickly, but you never know when you may need something.

Admit it. The whole process wasn't as bad as you thought it would be. Maybe you even had fun. Maybe you're such an expert now that you're helping your friends' kids through the process.

Send us your experiences

Most parents who go through the college admissions process learn a lot about themselves and their children. They also collect a lot of good stories along the way. No two college admissions journeys are alike.

Send us your experiences. We'd love to know what you encountered along the way. We'd also like to know what was most helpful about this book. Send any comments, good or bad, to:

The Parents' Guide to Surviving the College
   Admissions Process
c/o Citadel Press
120 Enterprise Ave.
Secaucus, NJ 07094

Extra Stuff

—

A Quick Reference
to some
very basic terms

ACT

The American College Testing program, which administers college entrance exams, similar to the SATs, in some parts of the country including the Midwest and the South.

Early Acceptance

An option offered by some colleges whereby the student is notified of the decision early, but with no requirement to accept the offer of admission.

Early Decision

An option offered by some colleges whereby students are notified early of the school's decision, with the stipulation that the student must accept the offer of admission and withdraw all other applications.

Early Notification

Same as early acceptance.

ETS

Educational Testing Service. The people in Princeton, New Jersey, who produce and administer the SATs.

FAF

Financial Aid Form. An application form put out by the College Scholarship Service of the College Board Admissions Testing Program of ETS. Required by some schools.

FAFSA

Free Application for Federal Student Aid. An application form used by all colleges, all federal financial aid programs, and some state aid programs.

Financial Aid

Financial assistance given to college students in the form of grants, loans, or work-study programs, awarded on the basis of need or merit.

Grants

Outright awards of money from colleges or other sources, based either on financial need or merit (academic, sports, music, etc.).

Information Session

Group sessions offered by many colleges that bring together applicants, their parents, and admissions counselors for a discussion about the college and its requirements for admission.

Loans

A variety of packages from the college, state or federal government, or other sources, which make money available to prospective students to help finance their education, with various methods of payback.

National Merit Scholarship

A program which awards scholarships to prospective college students based on their performance on the Preliminary Scholastic Assessment Test (PSAT).

Non-binding Early Decision

Same as early acceptance and early notification.

PSAT

Preliminary Scholastic Assessment Test. A shorter version of the SAT, usually given to students in their junior year of high school as practice for the SATs. Basis for awarding National Merit Scholarships.

Rolling Admission

An option offered by some colleges whereby applications are reviewed as they come in, and notification is on a rolling basis.

SAT-I

Scholastic Assessment Test. College entrance examination administered by the College Board Testing Program of the Educational Testing Service of Princeton, New Jersey, consisting of three hours of verbal and math questions. Required by many colleges (virtually all in the Northeast). Also referred to as SAT-I. Formerly known as the Scholastic Aptitude Test.

SAT-II

One-hour subject matter tests administered by the Educational Testing Service of Princeton, New Jersey. These tests are supposed to measure a student's knowledge in various subjects, e.g., English, history, mathematics, biology. Required for admission to the most selective colleges. Formerly known as Achievement tests.

Student Descriptive Questionnaire

Questions contained on the registration form for the SATs, intended to match a student's qualifications and preferences with colleges and career choices. The questionnaire is made available to schools receiving SAT score reports.

Work-Study

Financial aid awarded to students, usually on the basis of financial need, in the form of employment opportunities while attending college.

Timetable:
What to Do
and when to do it

Summer before junior year

- Begin to visit colleges
- Send away (or call) for college information
- Compile list of possible colleges

Junior year

Fall

- Register for and take preliminary standardized tests
- Keep working on your list of possible colleges

December

- Check SAT and ACT schedules and plan dates for spring

Spring

- Register for and take appropriate SAT/ACT tests

Summer before senior year

- Send away for applications
- Take more college trips
- Refine list of colleges
- Prepare your grid
- Complete first draft of essay

Senior year

Fall

- Keep refining list of colleges
- Register for and take appropriate SAT/ACT tests
- Finish essay
- Obtain letters of recommendation
- Complete and send in applications to schools with rolling admissions or early decision

December

- Complete balance of applications

January

- Complete and submit financial aid applications

Want More?

Buy a copy
for a desperate friend!

If you liked what
**The Parents' Guide to Surviving the
College Admissions Process**
did for you,
think how happy
you can make a friend.

Copies are now available by mailing this order form
along with your payment to:
**The Parents' Guide to Surviving the
College Admissions Process**
Citadel Press
120 Enterprise Avenue, Dept. B, Secaucus, NJ 07094

___ books at $9.95 per book $_____
NJ residents: add 6% sales tax per book $_____
Shipping/handling: $4 per book $_____
Total enclosed $_____

Please allow 4–6 weeks for delivery.
Please make check or money order payable to:
Citadel Press
For fastest service, or to charge your order to
MasterCard or Visa, call 1-800-447-BOOK.

Name _____

Address _____

City / State / Zip _____

Telephone (____) _____